American Indian Symbolism

By Manly P. Hall

Copyright © 2020 Lamp of Trismegistus. All rights reserved. No part of this publication may be reproduced or transmitted in any form or by any means, electronic or mechanical, including photocopying, recording, or by any information storage and retrieval system, without permission in writing from Lamp of Trismegistus. Reviewers may quote brief passages.

ISBN: 978-1-63118-463-5

Esoteric Classics

Other Books in this Series and Related Titles

American Indian Freemasonry by A. C. Parker (978-1-63118-460-4)

Crystal Vision Through Crystal Gazing by Achad (978-1-63118-455-0)

The Mysteries of Freemasonry & the Druids
by Albert G. Mackey, Manly P. Hall &c (978-1-63118-444-4)

The Legend of the Holy Grail and its Connection with Templars and Freemasons by A. E. Waite (978-1-63118-462-8)

Ancient Egyptian Mysteries and Hieroglyphics, Modern Freemasonry & Initiation of the Pyramid by various (978-1-63118-430-7)

Arcane Formulas or Mental Alchemy
by William Walker Atkinson (978-1-63118-459-8)

The Machinery of the Mind by Dion Fortune (978-1-63118-451-2)

Freemasonry and the Egyptian Mysteries
by C. W. Leadbeater (978-1-63118-456-7)

Lost Atlantis and the Gods of Antiquity & Plato's History of Atlantis
by Carolus Kiesewetterus &c (978-1-63118-431-4)

Plato and Platonism and Related Esoteric Essays
by Helena P. Blavatsky & others (978-1-63118-432-1)

The Secrets of Enoch by Enoch (978-1-63118-449-9)

The Rosicrucian Chemical Marriage
by Christian Rosenkreuz (978-1-63118-458-1)

Some Deeper Aspects of Masonic Symbolism
by A. E. Waite (978-1-63118-461-1)

The Kabbalah of Masonry & Related Writings
by W. W. Westcott, Eliphas Levi &c (978-1-63118-453-6)

Audio Versions are also Available on Audible and iTunes

Table of Contents

Introduction...7

American Indian Symbolism...9

The Popol Vuh...17

The Mysteries of Xibalba...21

Keys to the Mysteries of Xibalba...31

INTRODUCTION

The word "esoteric" can be difficult to define. Esotericism in general can be seen less as a system of beliefs and more as a category, which encompasses numerous, different systems of beliefs. It's a bit of juxtaposition, since the word "esoteric" indicates something that few people know about, while the term itself broadly covers numerous philosophies, practices, areas of study and belief systems.

In a greater sense, Esotericism acts as a storehouse for secret knowledge, which is often considered ancient (by *tradition, if not by fact*), passed down from generation to generation, in private. At various times in history, simply possessing the knowledge of some of these subjects, was considered illegal and a jailable offense, if discovered. This usually included such general topics as Alchemy, Qabalah, Hermeticism, Occultism, Ceremonial Magic, Astrology, Divination, Rosicrucianism and so on. Collectively, these areas of study were often referred to as the esoteric sciences.

Sometimes, the outer garment of a subject isn't esoteric, while what is hidden beneath it, is. As an example, Freemasonry isn't necessarily esoteric by nature (at *least not anymore*), but certain signs, passwords and handshakes given to the candidate during their initiation, are in fact, esoteric, in the sense that they are hidden from the general public.

Today, in the twenty-first century, such topics are readily available at bookstores across the country, and numerous mainsteam publishers offer beginners guides and coffee-table volumes on many of these subjects, intended for mass appeal. Books like *"The Secret"* have turned previously arcane topics into household knowledge. All that being the case, however, it isn't to say that there still aren't buried secrets to uncover, ancient wisdom being ignored and forgotten mysteries to be explored. In fact, it is often that we are only able to further our own studies by standing on the shoulders of these disappearing giants.

Lamp of Trismegistus is doing its part to help preserve humanity's esoteric history by making some of these classics available to those students who are seeking to unearth the knowledge of these ancient colossi.

So, be sure to check other titles from our *Esoteric Classics* series, as well as our *Occult Fiction, Theosophical Classics, Foundations of Freemasonry Series, Supernatural Fiction, Paranormal Research Series, Studies in Buddhism* and our *Christian Apocrypha Series*. You can also download the audio versions of most of these titles from iTunes or Audible, for learning on the go.

AMERICAN INDIAN SYMBOLISM

The North American Indian is by nature a symbolist, a mystic, and a philosopher. Like most aboriginal peoples, his soul was en rapport with the cosmic agencies manifesting about him. Not only did his Manidos control creation from their exalted seats above the clouds, but they also descended into the world of men and mingled with their red children. The gray clouds hanging over the horizon were the smoke from the calumets of the gods, who could build fires of petrified wood and use a comet for a flame. The American Indian peopled the forests, rivers, and sky with myriads of superphysical and invisible beings. There are legends of entire tribes of Indians who lived in lake bottoms; of races who were never seen in the daytime but who, coming forth from their hidden caves, roamed the earth at night and waylaid unwary travelers; also of Bat Indians, with human bodies and batlike wings, who lived in gloomy forests and inaccessible cliffs and who slept hanging head downward from great branches and outcroppings of rock. The red man's philosophy of elemental creatures is apparently the outcome of his intimate contact with Nature, whose inexplicable wonders become the generating cause of such metaphysical speculations.

In common with the early Scandinavians, the Indians of North America considered the earth (the Great Mother) to be an intermediate plane, bounded above by a heavenly sphere (the dwelling place of the Great Spirit) and below by a dark and terrifying subterranean world (the abode of shadows and of submundane powers). Like the Chaldeans, they divided the interval between the surface of earth and heaven into various strata, one consisting of clouds, another of the paths of the heavenly bodies, and so on. The underworld was similarly divided and like the Greek system represented to the initiated the House of the Lesser Mysteries. Those creatures capable of functioning in two or more elements were considered as messengers between the spirits of these various planes. The abode of the dead was presumed to be in a distant place: in the heavens above, the earth below, the distant corners of the world, or across wide seas. Sometimes a river flows between the world of the dead and that of the living, in this respect paralleling Egyptian, Greek, and Christian theology. To the Indian the number four has a peculiar sanctity, presumably because the Great Spirit created His universe in a square frame. This is suggestive of the veneration accorded the tetrad by the Pythagoreans, who held it to be a fitting symbol of the Creator. The legendary narratives of the strange adventures of intrepid heroes who while in the physical body penetrated the realms of the dead prove beyond question the presence of Mystery cults among the North American red men. Wherever the Mysteries were established they were recognized as the philosophic equivalents of death, for those passing through the rituals experienced all after-death conditions while still in the physical body. At the consummation of the ritual the initiate actually gained the ability to pass in and out of his physical body at will. This is the philosophic foundation for the allegories of adventures in the Indian Shadow Land, or World of Ghosts.

"From coast to coast," writes Hartley Burr Alexander, "the sacred Calumet is the Indian's altar, and its smoke is the proper offering to Heaven." (See Mythology of All Paces.) In the Notes on the same work is given the following description of the pipe ceremony:

"The master of ceremonies, again rising to his feet, filled and lighted the pipe of peace from his own fire. Drawing three whiffs, one after the other, he blew the first towards the zenith, the second towards the ground, and the third towards the Sun. By the first act he returned thanks to the Great Spirit for the preservation of his life during the past year, and for being permitted to be present at this council. By the second, he returned thanks to his Mother, the Earth, for her various productions which had ministered to his sustenance. And by the third, he returned thanks to the Sun for his never-failing light, ever shining upon all."

It was necessary for the Indian to secure the red stone for his calumet from the pipestone quarry where in some remote past the Great Spirit had come and, after fashioning with His own hands a great pipe, had smoked it toward the four corners of creation and thus instituted this most sacred ceremony. Scores of Indian tribes--some of them traveling thousands of miles--secured the sacred stone from this single quarry, where the mandate of the Great Spirit had decreed that eternal peace should reign.

The Indian does not worship the sun; he rather regards this shining orb as an appropriate symbol of the Great and

Good Spirit who forever radiates life to his red children. In Indian symbolism the serpent--especially the Great Serpent--corroborates other evidence pointing to the presence of the Mysteries on the North American Continent. The flying serpent is the Atlantean token of the initiate; the seven-headed snake represents the seven great Atlantean islands (the cities of Chibola?) and also the seven great prehistoric schools of esoteric philosophy. Moreover, who can doubt the presence of the secret doctrine in the Americas when he gazes upon the great serpent mound in Adams County, Ohio, where the huge reptile is represented as disgorging the Egg of Existence? Many American Indian tribes are reincarnationists, some are transmigrationists. They even called their children by the names supposed to have been borne by them in a former life. There is an account of an instance where a parent by inadvertence had given his infant the wrong name, whereupon the babe cried incessantly until the mistake had been rectified! The belief in reincarnation is also prevalent among the Eskimos. Aged Eskimos not infrequently kill themselves in order to reincarnate in the family of some newly married loved one.

The American Indians recognize the difference between the ghost and the actual soul of a dead person, a knowledge restricted to initiates of the Mysteries. In common with the Platonists they also understood the principles of an archetypal sphere wherein exist the patterns of all forms manifesting in the earth plane, The theory of Group, or Elder, Souls having supervision over the animal species is also shared by them. The red man's belief in guardian spirits would have warmed the heart of Paracelsus. When they attain the importance of being

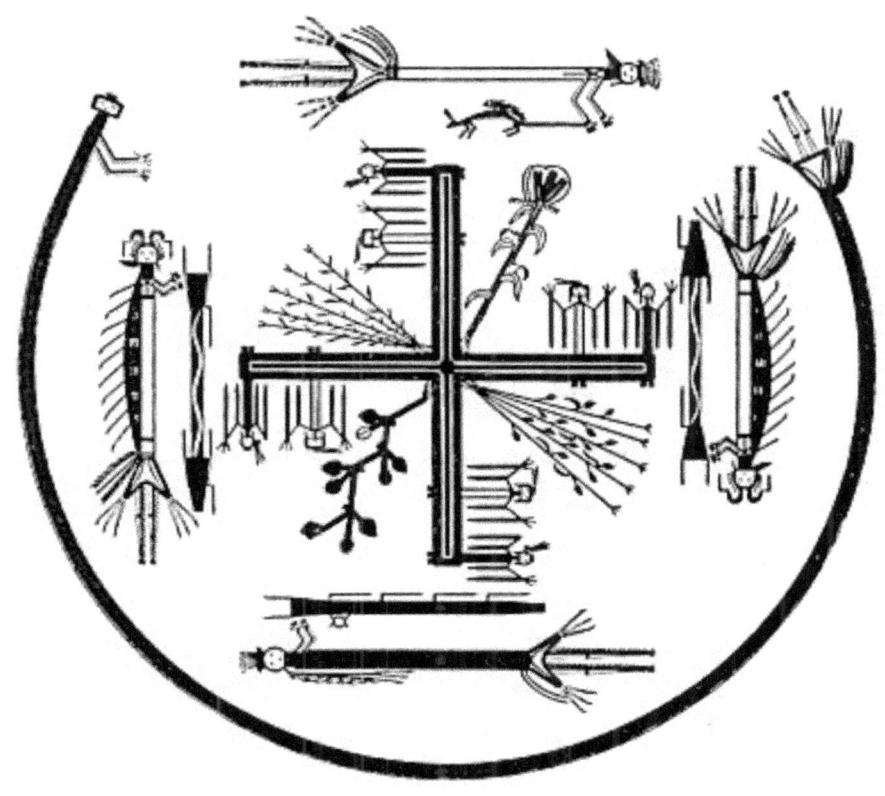

Navaho Sand Painting.[1]

---

[1] The Navaho dry or sand paintings are made by sprinkling varicolored ground pigment upon a base of smooth sand. The one here reproduced is encircled by the rainbow goddess, and portrays an episode from the Navaho cosmogony myth. According to Hasteen Klah, the Navaho sand priest who designed this painting, the Navahos do not believe in idolatry, hence they make no images of their gods, but perpetuate only the mental concept of them. Just as the gods draw pictures upon the moving clouds, so the priests make paintings on the sand, and when the purpose of the drawing has been fulfilled it is effaced by a sweep of the hand. According to this informant, the Zuni, Hopi, and Navaho nations had a common genesis; they all came out of the earth and then separated into three nations.

The Navahos first emerged about 3,000 years ago at a point now called La Platte Mountain in Colorado. The four mountains sacred to the Navahos are La Platte Mountain, Mount Taylor, Navaho Mountain, and San Francisco Mountain. While these three nations were under the earth four mountain ranges were below with them. The eastern mountains were white, the southern blue, the western yellow, and the northern black. The rise and fall of these mountains caused the alternation of day and night. When the white mountains rose it was day under the earth; when the yellow ones rose, twilight; the black mountains brought night, and the blue, dawn. Seven major deities were recognized by the Navahos, but Hasteen Klah was unable to say whether the protectors of entire clans or tribes, these guardians are called totems. In some tribes impressive ceremonies mark the occasion when the young men are sent out into the forest to fast and pray and there remain until their guardian spirit manifests to them. Whatever creature appears thereupon becomes their peculiar genius, to whom they appeal in time of trouble.

The outstanding hero of North American Indian folklore is Hiawatha, a name which, according to Lewis Spence, signifies "he who seeks the wampum-belt." Hiawatha enjoys the distinction of anticipating by several centuries the late Woodrow Wilson's cherished dream of a League of Nations. Following in the footsteps of Schoolcraft, Longfellow confused the historical Hiawatha of the Iroquois with Manabozho, a mythological hero of the Algonquins and Ojibwas. Hiawatha, a chief of the Iroquois, after many reverses and disappointments, succeeded in uniting the five great nations of the Iroquois into the "League of the Five Nations." The original purpose of the league--to abolish war by substituting councils of arbitration--

---

Indians related these deities to the planets. Bakochiddy, one of these seven major gods, was white in color with light reddish hair and gray eyes. His father was the sun ray and his mother the daylight. He ascended to heaven and in some respects his life parallels that of Christ. To avenge the kidnapping of his child, Kahothsode, a fish god, caused a great flood to arise. To escape destruction, the Zunis, Hopis, and Navahos ascended to the surface of the earth.

The sand painting here reproduced is part of the medicine series prepared far the healing of disease. In the healing ceremony the patient is placed upon the drawing, which is made in a consecrated hogan, and all outsiders excluded. The sacred swastika in the center of the drawing is perhaps the most nearly universal of religious emblems and represents the four corners of the world. The two hunchback god, at the right and left assume their appearance by reason of the great clouds borne upon their backs. In Navaho religious art, male divinities are always shown with circular heads and female divinities with square heads.

was not wholly successful, but the power of the "Silver Chain" conferred upon the Iroquois a solidarity attained by no other confederacy of North American Indians. Hiawatha, however, met the same opposition which has confronted every great idealist, irrespective of time or race. The shamans turned their magic against him and, according to one legend, created an evil bird which, swooping down from heaven, tore his only daughter to pieces before his eyes. When Hiawatha, after accomplishing his mission, had sailed away in his self-propelled canoe along the path of the sunset, his people realized the true greatness of their benefactor and elevated him to the dignity of a demigod. In Longfellow's Song of Hiawatha the poet has cast the great Indian statesman in a charming setting of magic and enchantment; yet through the maze of symbol and allegory is ever faintly visible the figure of Hiawatha the initiate--the very personification of the red man and his philosophy.

THE POPOL VUH

No other sacred book sets forth so completely as the *Popol Vuh* the initiatory rituals of a great school of mystical philosophy. This volume alone is sufficient to establish incontestably the philosophical excellence of the red race.

"The Red 'Children of the Sun,'" writes James Morgan Pryse, "do not worship the One God. For them that One God is absolutely impersonal, and all the Forces emanated from that One God are personal. This is the exact reverse of the popular western conception of a personal God and impersonal working forces in nature. Decide for yourself which of these beliefs is the more philosophical. These Children of the Sun adore the Plumèd Serpent, who is the messenger of the Sun. He was the God Quetzalcoatl in Mexico, Gucumatz in Quiché; and in Peru he was called Amaru. From the latter name comes our word America. Amaruca is, literally translated, 'Land of the Plumèd Serpent.' The priests of this God of Peace, from their chief centre in the Cordilleras, once ruled both Americas. All the Red men who have remained true to the ancient religion are still under their sway. One of their strong centres was in Guatemala, and of their Order was the author of the book called *Popol Vuh*. In the Quiché tongue Gucumatz is the exact equivalent of Quetzalcoatl in the Nahuatl language; quetzal, the bird of Paradise; coatl, serpent--'the Serpent veiled in plumes of the paradise-bird'!"

The *Popol Vuh* was discovered by Father Ximinez in the seventeenth century. It was translated into French by Brasseur de Bourbourg and published in 1861. The only complete English translation is that by Kenneth Sylvan Guthrie, which ran through the early files of The Word magazine and which is used as the basis of this article. A portion of the *Popol Vuh* was translated into English, with extremely valuable commentaries, by James Morgan Pryse, but unfortunately his translation was never completed. The second book of the *Popol Vuh* is largely devoted to the initiatory rituals of the Quiché nation. These ceremonials are of first importance to students of Masonic symbolism and mystical philosophy, since they establish beyond doubt the existence of ancient and divinely instituted Mystery schools on the American Continent.

Lewis Spence, in describing the *Popol Vuh*, gives a number of translations of the title of the manuscript itself. Passing over the renditions, "The Book of the Mat" and "The Record of the Community," he considers it likely that the correct title is "The Collection of Written Leaves," Popol signifying the "prepared bark" and Vuh, "paper" or "book" from the verb uoch, to write. Dr. Guthrie interprets the words *Popol Vuh* to mean "The Senate Book," or "The Book of the Holy Assembly"; Brasseur de Bourbourg calls it "The Sacred Book"; and Father Ximinez designates the volume "The National Book." In his articles on the *Popol Vuh* appearing in the fifteenth volume of Lucifer, James Morgan Pryse, approaching the subject from the standpoint of the mystic, calls this work "The Book of the Azure Veil." In the *Popol Vuh* itself the ancient records from which the Christianized Indian who compiled it derived his material are referred to as "The Tale of Human Existence in the Land of Shadows, and, How Man Saw Light and Life."

The meager available native records contain abundant evidence that the later civilizations of Central and South America were hopelessly dominated by the black arts of their priestcrafts. In the convexities of their magnetized mirrors the Indian sorcerers captured the intelligences of elemental beings and, gazing into the depths of these abominable devices, eventually made the scepter subservient to the wand. Robed in garments of sable hue, the neophytes in their search for truth were led by their sinister guides through the confused passageways of necromancy. By the left-hand path they descended into the somber depths of the infernal world, where they learned to endow stones with the power of speech and to subtly ensnare the minds of men with their chants and fetishes. As typical of the perversion which prevailed, none could achieve to the greater Mysteries until a human being had suffered immolation at his hand and the bleeding heart of the victim had been elevated before the leering face of the stone idol fabricated by a priestcraft the members of which realized more fully than they dared to admit the true nature of the man-made demon. The sanguinary and indescribable rites practiced by many of the Central American Indians may represent remnants of the later Atlantean perversion of the ancient sun Mysteries. According to the secret tradition, it was during the later Atlantean epoch that black magic and sorcery dominated the esoteric schools, resulting in the bloody sacrificial rites and gruesome idolatry which ultimately overthrew the Atlantean empire and even penetrated the Aryan religious world.

THE MYSTERIES OF XIBALBA

The princes of Xibalba (so the *Popol Vuh* recounts) sent their four owl messengers to Hunhun-ahpu and Vukub-hunhun-ahpu, ordering them to come at once to the place of initiation in the fastnesses of the Guatemalan mountains. Failing in the tests imposed by the princes of Xibalba, the two brothers-- according to the ancient custom--paid with their lives for their shortcomings. Hunhun-ahpu and Vukub-hunhun-ahpu were buried together, but the head of Hunhun-ahpu was placed among the branches of the sacred calabash tree which grew in the middle of the road leading to the awful Mysteries of Xibalba. Immediately the calabash tree covered itself with fruit and the head of Hunhun-ahpu "showed itself no more; for it reunited itself with the other fruits of the calabash tree." Now Xquiq was the virgin daughter of prince Cuchumaquiq. From her father she had learned of the marvelous calabash tree, and desiring to possess some of its fruit, she journeyed alone to the somber place where it grew. When Xquiq put forth her hand to pick the fruit of the tree, some saliva from the mouth of Hunhun-ahpu fell into it and the head spoke to Xquiq, saying: "This saliva and froth is my posterity which I have just given you. Now my head will cease to speak, for it is only the head of a corpse, which has no more flesh."

Following the admonitions of Hunhun-ahpu, the young girl returned to her home. Her father, Cuchumaquiq, later discovering that she was about to become a mother, questioned her concerning the father of her child. Xquiq replied that the child was begotten while she was gazing upon the head of Hunhun-ahpu in the calabash tree and that she had known no man. Cuchumaquiq, refusing to believe her story, at the instigation of the princes of Xibalba, demanded her heart in an urn. Led away by her executioners, Xquiq pleaded with them to spare her life, which they agreed to do, substituting for her heart the fruit of a certain tree (rubber) whose sap was red and of the consistency of blood. When the princes of Xibalba placed the supposed heart upon the coals of the altar to be consumed, they were all amazed by the perfume which rose therefrom, for they did not know that they were burning the fruit of a fragrant plant.

Xquiq gave birth to twin sons, who were named Hunahpu and Xbalanque and whose lives were dedicated to avenging the deaths of Hunhun-ahpu and Vukub-hunhun-ahpu. The years passed, and the two boys grew up to manhood and great were their deeds. Especially did they excel in a certain game called tennis but somewhat resembling hockey. Hearing of the prowess of the youths, the princes of Xibalba asked: "Who, then, are those who now begin again to play over our heads, and who do not scruple to shake (the earth)? Are not Hunhun-ahpu and Vukub-hunhun-ahpu dead, who wished to exalt themselves before our face?" So the princes of Xibalba sent for the two youths, Hunahpu and Xbalanque, that they might destroy them also in the seven days of the Mysteries. Before departing, the two brothers bade farewell to their grandmother, each planting in the midst of the house a cane plant, saying that as long as the cane lived she would know that

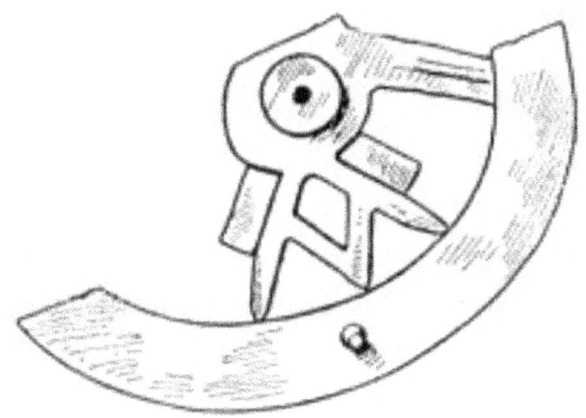

Fragment of Indian Pottery.[2]

they were alive. "O, our grandmother, O, our mother, do not weep; behold the sign of our word which remains with you." Hunahpu and Xbalanque then departed, each with his sabarcan (blowpipe), and for many days they journeyed along the perilous trail, descending through tortuous ravines and along precipitous cliffs, past strange birds and boiling springs, cowards the sanctuary of Xibalba.

The actual ordeals of the Xibalbian Mysteries were seven in number. As a preliminary the two adventurers crossed a river of mud and then a stream of blood, accomplishing these difficult feats by using their sabarcans as bridges. Continuing on their way, they reached a point where four roads converged--a black road, a white road, a red road, and a green road. Now Hunahpu and Xbalanque knew that their first test would

---

[2] This curious fragment was found four feet under the ground beneath a trash pile of broken early Indian pottery not far from the Casa Grande ruins in Arizona. It is significant because of its striking to the Masonic compass and square. Indian baskets pottery, and blankets frequertly bear ornamental designs of especial Masonic and philosophic interest.

consist of being able to discriminate between the princes of Xibalba and the wooden effigies robed to resemble them; also that they must call each of the princes by his correct name without having been given the information. To secure this information, Hunahpu pulled a hair from his leg, which hair then became a strange insect called Xan; buzzing along the black road, the Xan entered the council chamber of the princes of Xibalba and stung the leg of the figure nearest the door, which it discovered to be a manikin. By the same artifice the second figure was proved to be of wood, but upon stinging the third, there was an immediate response. By stinging each of the twelve assembled princes in turn the insect thus discovered each one's name, for the princes called each other by name in discussing the cause of the mysterious bites. Having secured the desired information in this novel manner, the insect then flew back to Hunahpu and Xbalanque, who thus fortified, fearlessly approached the threshold of Xibalba and presented themselves to the twelve assembled princes.

When told to adore the king, Hunahpu and Xbalanque laughed, for they knew that the figure pointed out to them was the lifeless manikin. The young adventurers thereupon addressed the twelve princes by name thus: "Hail, Hun-came; hail, Vukub-came; hail, Xiquiripat; hail, Cuchumaquiq; hail, Ahalpuh; hail, Ahalcana; hail, Chamiabak; hail, Chamiaholona; hail, Quiqxic; hail, Patan; hail, Quiqre; hail, Quiqrixqaq." When invited by the Xibalbians to seat themselves upon a great stone bench, Hunahpu and Xbalanque declined to do so, declaring that they well knew the stone to be heated so that they would he burned to death if they sat upon it. The princes of Xibalba then ordered Hunahpu and Xbalanque to rest for the night in the House of Shadows. This completed the first degree of the Xibalbian Mysteries.

The second trial was given in the House of Shadows, where to each of the candidates was brought a pine torch and a cigar, with the injunction that both must be kept alight throughout the entire night and yet each must be returned the next morning unconsumed. Knowing that death was the alternative to failure in the test, the young men burnt aras-feathers in place of the pine splinters (which they closely resemble) and also put fireflies on the tips of the cigars. Seeing the lights, those who watched felt certain that Hunahpu and Xbalanque had fallen into the trap, but when morning came the torches and cigars were returned to the guards unconsumed and still burning. In amazement and awe, the princes of Xibalba gazed upon the unconsumed splinters and cigars, for never before had these been returned intact.

The third ordeal took place presumably in a cavern called the House of Spears. Here hour after hour the youths were forced to defend themselves against the strongest and most skillful warriors armed with spears. Hunahpu and Xbalanque pacified the spearmen, who thereupon ceased attacking them. They then turned their attention to the second and most difficult part of the test: the production of four vases of the rarest flowers but which they were not permitted to leave the temple to gather. Unable to pass the guards, the two young men secured the assistance of the ants. These tiny creatures, crawling into the gardens of the temple, brought back the blossoms so that by morning the vases were filled. When Hunahpu and Xbalanque presented the flowers to the twelve princes, the latter, in amazement, recognized the blossoms as having been filched from their own private gardens. In consternation, the princes of Xibalba then counseled together how they could destroy the intrepid neophytes and forthwith prepared for them the next ordeal.

For their fourth test, the two brothers were made to enter the House of Cold, where they remained for an entire night. The princes of Xibalba considered the chill of the icy cavern to be unbearable and it is described as "the abode of the frozen winds of the North." Hunahpu and Xbalanque, however, protected themselves from the deadening influence of the frozen air by building fires of pine cones, whose warmth caused the spirit of cold to leave the cavern so that the youths were not dead but full of life when day dawned. Even greater than before was the amazement of the princes of Xibalba when Hunahpu and Xbalanque again entered the Hall of Assembly in the custody of their guardians.

The fifth ordeal was also of a nocturnal nature. Hunahpu and Xbalanque were ushered into a great chamber which was immediately filled with ferocious tigers. Here they were forced to remain throughout the night. The young men tossed bones to the tigers, which they ground to pieces with their strong jaws. Gazing into the House of the Tigers, the princes of Xibalba beheld the animals chewing the bones and said one to the other: "They have at last learned (to know the power of Xibalba), and they have given themselves up to the beasts." But when at dawn

Midewiwin Record on Birch Bark.[3]

---

[3] The birch-bark roll is one of the most sacred possessions of an initiate of the Midewiwin, or Grand Medicine Society, of the Ojibwas. Concerning these rolls, Colonel Carrick Mallery writes: "To persons acquainted with secret societies, a good comparison for the Midewiwin charts would be what is called a trestleboard of a Masonic order, which is printed and published and publicly exposed without exhibiting any secrets of the order; yet it is not only significant, but useful to the esoteric in assistance to their memory as to the details of ceremony." A most complete and trustworthy account of the Midewiwin is that given by W. J. Hoffman in the Seventh Annual Report of the Bureau of Ethnology. He writes:

The Midewiwin--Society of the Mide or Shaman--consists of an indefinite number of Mide of both sexes. The society is graded into four separate and distinct degrees, although there is a general impression prevailing even among certain members that any degree beyond the first is practically a mere repetition. The greater power attained by one in making advancement depends upon the fact of his having submitted to 'being shot at with the medicine sacks' in the hands of the officiating priests. * * * It has always been customary for the Mide priests to preserve birch-bark records, bearing delicate incised lines to represent pictorially the ground plan of the number of degrees to which the owner is entitled. Such records or charts are sacred and are never exposed to the public view."

The two rectangular diagrams represent two degrees of the Mide lodge and the straight line through the center the spiritual path, or "straight and narrow way," running through the degrees. The lines running tangent to the central Path signify temptations, and the faces at the termini of the lines are manidos, or powerful spirits. Writing of the Midewiwin, Schoolcraft, the great authority on the American Indian, says: "In the society of the Midewiwin the object is to teach the higher doctrines of spiritual existence, its nature and mode of existence, and the influence it exercises among men. It is an association of men who profess the highest knowledge known to the tribes."

According to legend, Manabozho, the great Rabbit, who was a servant of Dzhe Manido, the Good Spirit, gazing down upon the progenitors of the Ojibwas and perceiving them to be without spiritual knowledge, instructed an otter in the mysteries of Midewiwin. Manabozho built a Midewigan and initiated the otter, shooting the sacred Migis (a small shell, the sacred symbol of the Mide) into the body of the otter. He then conferred immortality upon the animal, and entrusted to it the secrets of the Grand

Hunahpu and Xbalanque emerged from the House of the Tigers unharmed, the Xibalbians cried: "Of what race are those?" for they could not understand how any man could escape the tigers' fury. Then the princes of Xibalba prepared for the two brothers a new ordeal.

The sixth test consisted of remaining from sunset to sunrise in the House of Fire. Hunahpu and Xbalanque entered a large apartment arranged like a furnace. On every side the flames arose and the air was stifling; so great was the heat that those who entered this chamber could survive only a few moments. But at sunrise when the doors of the furnace were opened, Hunahpu and Xbalanque came forth unscorched by the fury of the flames. The princes of Xibalba, perceiving how the two intrepid youths had survived every ordeal prepared for their destruction, were filled with fear lest all the secrets of Xibalba should fall into the hands of Hunahpu and Xbalanque. So they prepared the last ordeal, an ordeal yet more terrible than any which had gone before, certain that the youths could not withstand this crucial test.

The seventh ordeal took place in the House of the Bats. Here in a dark subterranean labyrinth lurked many strange and odious creatures of destruction. Huge bars fluttered dismally through the corridors and hung with folded wings from the

---

Medicine Society. The ceremony of initiation is preceded by sweat baths and consists chiefly of overcoming the influences of evil manidos. The initiate is also instructed in the art of healing and (judging from Plate III of Mr. Hoffman's article) a knowledge of directionalizing the forces moving through the vital centers of the human body. Though the cross is an important symbol in the Midewiwin rites, it is noteworthy that the Mide Priests steadfastly refused to give up their religion and be converted to Christianity.

carvings on the walls and ceilings. Here also dwelt Camazotz, the God of Bats, a hideous monster with the body of a man and the wings and head of a bat. Camazotz carried a great sword and, soaring through the gloom, decapitated with a single sweep of his blade any unwary wanderers seeking to find their way through the terror-filled chambers. Xbalanque passed successfully through this horrifying test, but Hunahpu, caught off his guard, was beheaded by Camazotz.

Later, Hunahpu was restored to life by magic, and the two brothers, having thus foiled every attempt against their lives by the Xibalbians, in order to better avenge the murder of Hunhun-ahpu and Vukub-hunhun-ahpu, permitted themselves to be burned upon a funeral pyre. Their powdered bones were then cast into a river and immediately became two great man-fishes. Later taking upon themselves the forms of aged wanderers, they danced for the Xibalbians and wrought strange miracles. Thus one would cut the other to pieces and with a single word resurrect him, or they would burn houses by magic and then instantly rebuild them. The fame of the two dancers--who were in reality Hunahpu and Xbalanque--finally came to the notice of the twelve princes of Xibalba, who thereupon desired these two miracle-workers to perform their strange fears before them. After Hunahpu and Xbalanque had slain the dog of the princes and restored it to life, had burned the royal palace and instantly rebuilt it, and given other demonstrations of their magical powers, the monarch of the Xibalbians asked the magicians to destroy him and restore him also to life. So Hunahpu and Xbalanque slew the princes of Xibalba but did not return them to life, thereby avenging the murder of

Hunhun-ahpu and Vukub-hunhun-ahpu. These heroes later ascended to heaven, where they became the celestial lights.

KEYS TO THE MYSTERIES OF XIBALBA

"Do not these initiations," writes Le Plongeon, "vividly recall to mind what Henoch said he saw in his visions? That blazing house of crystal, burning hot and icy cold--that place where were the bow of fire, the quiver of arrows, the sword of fire--that other where he had to cross the babbling stream, and the river of fire-and those extremities of the Earth full of all kinds of huge beasts and birds--or the habitation where appeared one of great glory sitting upon the orb of the sun-- and, lastly, does not the tamarind tree in the midst of the earth, that he was told was the Tree of Knowledge, find its simile in the calabash tree, in the middle of the road where those of Xibalba placed the head of Hunhun Ahpu, after sacrificing him for having failed to support the first trial of the initiation? * * * These were the awful ordeals that the candidates for initiation into the sacred mysteries had to pass through in Xibalba. Do they not seem an exact counterpart of what happened in a milder form at the initiation into the Eleusinian mysteries? and also the greater mysteries of Egypt, from which these were copied? Does not the recital of what the candidates to the mysteries in Xibalba were required to know, before being admitted, * * * recall to mind the wonderful similar feats said to be performed by the Mahatmas, the Brothers in India, and of several of the passages of the book of Daniel, who had been initiated to the mysteries of the Chaldeans or Magi which, according to Eubulus, were divided into three classes or genera, the highest being the most learned?" (See Sacred Mysteries among the Mayas and the Quiches.)

In his introductory notes to the *Popol Vuh*, Dr. Guthrie presents a number of important parallelisms between this sacred book of the Quichés and the sacred writings of other great civilizations. In the tests through which Hunahpu and Xbalanque are forced to pass he finds the following analogy with the signs of the zodiac as employed in the Mysteries of the Egyptians, Chaldeans, and Greeks:

> "Aries, crossing the river of mud. Taurus, crossing the river of blood. Gemini, detecting the two dummy kings. Cancer, the House of Darkness. Leo, the House of Spears. Virgo, the House of Cold (the usual trip to Hell). Libra, the House of Tigers (feline poise). Scorpio, the House of Fire. Sagittarius, the House of Bats, where the God Camazotz decapitates one of the heroes. Capricorn, the burning on the scaffold (the dual Phœnix). Aquarius, their ashes being scattered in a river. Pisces, their ashes turning into man-fishes, and later back into human form."

It would seem more appropriate to assign the river of blood to Aries and that of mud to Taurus, and it is not at all improbable that in the ancient form of the legend the order of the rivers was reversed. Dr. Guthrie's most astonishing conclusion is his effort to identify Xibalba with the ancient continent of Atlantis. He sees in the twelve princes of Xibalba the rulers of the Atlantean empire, and in the destruction of these princes by the magic of Hunahpu and Xbalanque an allegorical depiction of the tragic end of Atlantis. To the initiated, however, it is evident that Atlantis is simply a symbolic figure in which is set forth the mystery of origins.

Concerned primarily with the problems of mystical anatomy, Mr. Pryse relates the various symbols described in the *Popol Vuh* to the occult centers of consciousness in the human body. Accordingly, he sees in the elastic ball the pineal gland and in Hunahpu and Xbalanque the dual electric current directed along the spinal column. Unfortunately, Mr. Pryse did not translate that portion of the *Popol Vuh* dealing directly with the initiatory ceremonial. Xibalba he considers to be the shadowy or etheric sphere which, according to the Mystery teachings, was located within the body of the planet itself. The fourth book of the *Popol Vuh* concludes with an account of the erection of a majestic temple, all white, where was preserved a secret black divining stone, cubical in shape. Gucumatz (or Quetzalcoatl) partakes of many of the attributes of King Solomon: the account of the temple building in the *Popol Vuh* is a reminder of the story of Solomon's Temple, and undoubtedly has a similar significance. Brasseur de Bourbourg was first attracted to the study of religious parallelisms in the *Popol Vuh* by the fact that the temple together with the black stone which it contained, was named the Caabaha, a name astonishingly similar to that of the Temple, or Caaba, which contains the sacred black stone of Islam.

The exploits of Hunahpu and Xbalanque take place before the actual creation of the human race and therefore are to be considered essentially as spiritual mysteries. Xibalba doubtless signifies the inferior universe of Chaldean and Pythagorean philosophy; the princes of Xibalba are the twelve Governors of the lower universe; and the two dummies or manikins in their midst may be interpreted as the two false signs of the ancient zodiac inserted in the heavens to make the astronomical Mysteries incomprehensible to the profane. The descent of Hunahpu and Xbalanque into the subterranean kingdom of Xibalba by crossing over the rivers on bridges made from their blowguns has a subtle analogy to the descent of the spiritual nature of man into the physical body through certain superphysical channels that may be likened to the blowguns or tubes. The sabarcan is also an appropriate emblem of the spinal cord and the power resident within its tiny central opening. The two youths are invited to play the "Game of Life" with the Gods of Death, and only with the aid of supernatural power imparted to them by the "Sages" can they triumph over these gloomy lords. The tests represent the soul wandering through the sub-zodiacal realms of the created universe; their final victory over the Lords of Death represents the ascension of the spiritual and illumined consciousness from the tower nature which has been wholly consumed by the fire of spiritual purification.

That the Quichés possessed the keys to the mystery of regeneration is evident from an analysis of the symbols appearing upon the images of their priests and gods. In Vol. II of the Anales del Museo Nacional de México is reproduced the head of an image generally considered to represent Quetzalcoatl. The sculpturing is distinctly Oriental in character and on the crown of the head appear both the thousand-petaled sunburst of spiritual illumination and the serpent of the liberated spinal fire. The Hindu chakra is unmistakable and it frequently appears in the religious art of the three Americas. One of the carved monoliths of Central America is adorned with the heads of two elephants with their drivers. No such animals have existed in the Western Hemisphere since prehistoric times and it is evident that the carvings are the result of contact with the distant continent of Asia. Among the Mysteries of the Central American Indians is a remarkable doctrine concerning the consecrated mantles or, as they were called in Europe, magic capes. Because their glory was fatal to mortal vision, the gods, when appearing to the initiated priests, robed themselves in these mantles, Allegory and fable likewise are the mantles with which the secret doctrine is ever enveloped. Such a magic cape of concealment is the *Popol Vuh*, and deep within its folds sits the god of Quiché philosophy. The massive pyramids, temples, and monoliths of Central America may be likened also to the feet of gods, whose upper parts are enshrouded in magic mantles of invisibility.

www.ingramcontent.com/pod-product-compliance
Lightning Source LLC
LaVergne TN
LVHW041503070426
835507LV00009B/786